The Light Shining in Our Hearts

Tracey Hunter

Illustrated by Jennifer Gillies

Published in 2023 by The Light Shining in Our Hearts

Copyright © 2023 Tracey Hunter

Tracey Hunter has asserted her right to be identified as the author of this Work in accordance with the Copyright, Designs and Patents Act 1988

ISBN Paperback: 978-1-7393274-0-8
Ebook: 978-1-7393274-1-5

All rights reserved. No part of this publication may be reproduced, stored in a retrieval system, or transmitted in any form or by any means, electronic, mechanical, photocopying, recording or otherwise, without the prior permission of the copyright owner.

All characters and events in this publication, other than those clearly in the public domain, are fictitious and any resemblance to real persons, living or dead, is purely coincidental.

A CIP catalogue copy of this book can be found in the British Library.

Published with the help of Indie Authors World
www.indieauthorsworld.com

May your life always be surrounded by light and love

Tracy
x

This book is dedicated to my children Janey and Robbie, my mum, Patsy, and to Conor.

In memory of my daughter Cora, who shows me the light.

Behold Thy Daughter

She Hath the Wind in her Hands

Cora was a very happy wee girl.

You melted into her big, blue eyes.

She loved being alive.

Her invisible touch reached right
into your heart.

Her squeals of delight filled you with warmth
and love and joy —

love given freely and shared with all she met.

Cora lived near the park.

One of her favourite times was when she took her dog, Dougal, for a walk there.

She loved to watch him run for sticks.

He never brought them back.

He never did what Mummy said.

She loved to play with her best friends, their names were Fiona, Ian and Julie.

She loved to play in the cupboards.

She loved to read her books.

She loved to eat.

She loved to watch the Blue Tits eat the coconut from the tree.

One day she had to go to the hospital.

She was very ill, Mummy and Daddy felt very sad.

The doctors told them that Cora could come home to die.

Mummy and Daddy felt happy because Cora could come back to her own house.

Cora knew she was home: she heard the Blue Tits singing on the windowsill.

She smelled the freesia beside her bed.

She felt Dougal lick her face.

Then one day she died.

Mummy and Daddy cried and cried and cried, inside and out.

They thought they had lost Cora forever.

All of her family and friends missed her so much, everything felt empty.

The world looked different, and time went on and on.

One day Julie and Ian went to the park to play on the swings.

Cora was there too: she danced among the leaves.

Mummy never saw her: she was so blinded she saw nothing.

Ian and Julie knew she was there.

Fiona cried one day, the clouds stopped her seeing Cora.

She let her balloon fly up into the sky, it was for Cora to play with.

Everyone thought of Cora: ripples of her love were felt everywhere.

Mummy and Daddy felt Cora inside their hearts and the light shone through.

The white light of the candle brought love.

Janey was born as if a butterfly of hope was blossoming.

Soon after Robbie arrived,

like an angel from the skies.

Life and laughter filled the house.

Dougal still did what suited him best.

Cora's life taught Mummy and Daddy how precious Janey and Robbie are.

How precious all life is.

When Janey, Robbie and their friends go to the park to play, Cora is there.

She is the wind that flies the kite.

She is the Robin singing on the fence.

She is the Swallow gliding through the air on a summer's evening.

She is the pure, white snowdrop peeping through the frosty ground.

She is the purple crocus bursting open.

She is the sun glistening on the sea.

She is the pink blossom that carpets the grove.

She is the midnight light in the sky
on a clear night.

When you look up at the moon and the stars,
Cora is there.

She is your friend by your side
forever and ever.

She plays with you, watches over you and helps
you when you need her.

Her love is every colour and shade of the
rainbow she sends you.

Some days Mummy and Daddy miss her; it
hurts not to be able to hold her and
watch her grow.

But Janey and Robbie know Cora,

and Cora knows Janey and Robbie.

We can't always see or feel her, but she's there.

She is the light shining in our hearts forever.

Our love never dies.

It is unending, the gift of life is always here.

Acknowledgements

I would like to thank my family and friends who have supported me unconditionally throughout the years. A heartfelt thank you to everyone who generously donated money, and to Indie Authors World for believing in this book and making it a reality.

A special acknowledgment to Jennifer who illustrated Cora's book so beautifully and harmoniously.

About Tracey

Tracey Hunter trained as a social worker in 1981. In a career spanning over forty years, she has worked with children, young adults and older people in Glasgow, the Scottish Borders, Bradford and the Southern Hebrides. She spent many years working with 'Looked After' children and young people and currently supports 'Unpaid Carers'.

In 1987, her first daughter Cora died in a tragic accident when she was fourteen months old. Since then, a large part of her life's work has been to encourage discussions about death, loss and separation, and to help people find meaning in their lives — even in the depths of grief.

She supported bereaved parents in Glasgow in the 1990s as a member of the peer support group 'The Compassionate Friends'. Through this work, she realised we are never alone in our grief, and made it her mission to support others to find a path through the darkness.

The Light Shining in our Hearts was first written for Cora's two siblings in 1991.

Tracey moved to Islay in 2008, where she enjoys walking, combing the beach and exploring the island's natural beauty. She is a keen baker and cook, and loves to share food with family and friends.

Tracey's website is: lightinourhearts.com

Milton Keynes UK
Ingram Content Group UK Ltd.
UKHW050327030823
426220UK00004B/33